Lots of

By Liza Charlesworth

ISBN: 978-1-339-02670-1

Art Director: Tannaz Fassihi; Designer: Tanya Chernyak
Photos ©: pp2, 8: mezzotint/Shutterstock.com. All other photos © Getty Images.
Copyright © Liza Charlesworth. All rights reserved. Published by Scholastic Inc.

3 4 5 6 7 8 9 10   68   32 31 30 29 28 27 26 25 24

Printed in Jiaxing, China. First printing, August 2023.

■SCHOLASTIC

Spots, spots, spots!
The dog has a stick
and lots of spots.

The big cat steps on rocks.
Can you see its spots?

The red bug stands on a stem.
It has six black spots.

Is the pig still in the grass? Yes!
It has ten big spots.

See the spots on the spider.
Spin, spin, spin!
It will not stop.

See the spots on the frog.
Hop hop, hop!
It can hop fast.

Spots, spots, spots!
A lot of animals have spots.
Spots are just the best!